Reading STREET

Scott Foresman
Graphic Organizer Book
for Grades 2–3

ISBN: 0-328-14596-3

6 7 8 9 10 V084 12 11 10 09 08 07

Editorial Offices: Glenview, Illinois • Parsippany, New Jersey • New York, New York
Sales Offices: Needham, Massachusetts • Duluth, Georgia • Glenview, Illinois
Coppell, Texas • Sacramento, California • Mesa, Arizona

Contents

Story Prediction from Previewing

Title _____

Read the title and look at the pictures in the story.
What do you think a problem in the story might be?

I think a problem might be _____

_____

_____

After reading _____,
draw a picture of one of the problems in the story.

┌───┐
│   │
│   │
│   │
│   │
│   │
│   │
│   │
│   │
│   │
│   │
└───┘

Story Prediction from Vocabulary

Title and Story Words

Read the title and the story words.
What do you think this story might be about?

I think this story might be about _____

_____

_____

After reading _____,
draw a picture that shows what the story is about.

K-W-L Chart

Topic _____

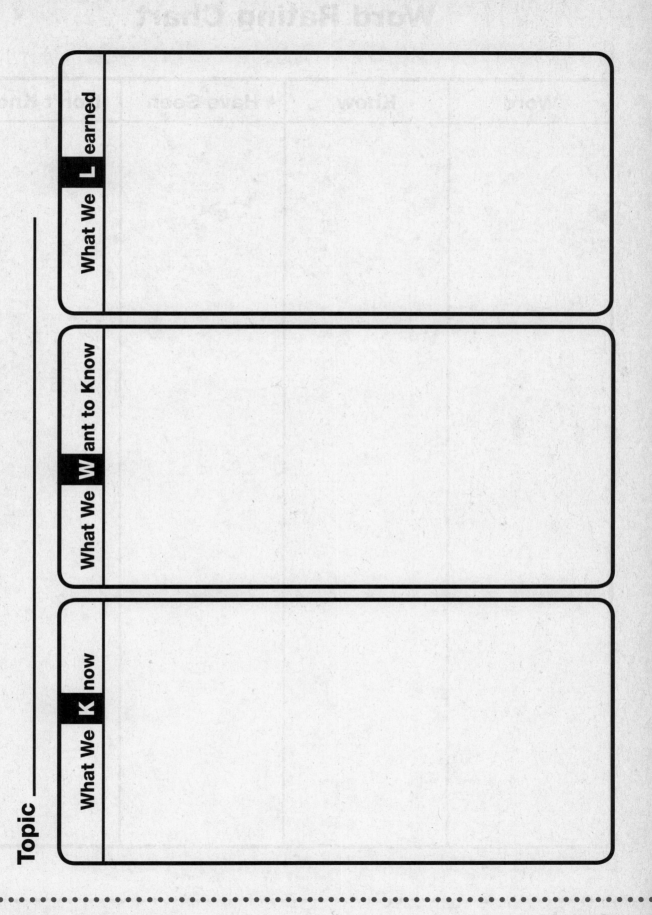

What We **K** now	What We **W** ant to Know	What We **L** earned

Word Rating Chart

Word	Know	Have Seen	Don't Know

Vocabulary Frame

Word

Association or Symbol

Predicted definition: _____

_____

One good sentence:

_____

_____

_____

Verified definition: _____

_____

_____

Another good sentence:

_____

_____

_____

Story Predictions Chart

Title _____

What might happen?	What clues do I have?	What did happen?

Story Sequence A

Title _____

Beginning

Middle

End

Story Sequence B

Title	
Characters	**Setting**

Events
1. First

2. Next

3. Then

4. Last

Story Sequence C

Title

Characters

Problem

Events

_____

_____

_____

_____

_____

_____

_____

Solution

Story Elements

Title _____

This story is about _____

_____
(name the characters)

This story takes place _____

_____
(where and when)

The action begins when _____

_____

Then, _____

_____

Next, _____

_____

After that, _____

_____

The story ends when _____

_____

Theme: _____

Question the Author

Title _____

Author _____ **Page** _____

1. What does the author tell you?	
2. Why do you think the author tells you that?	
3. Does the author say it clearly?	
4. What would make it clearer?	
5. How would you say it instead?	

Book Report

Title _____

Author _____

Illustrator _____

Setting _____

Characters _____

Our Favorite Parts _____

Story Comparison

Title A _____   Title B _____

_____   _____

Characters

Characters

Setting

Setting

Events

Events

Web A

Web B

Main Idea

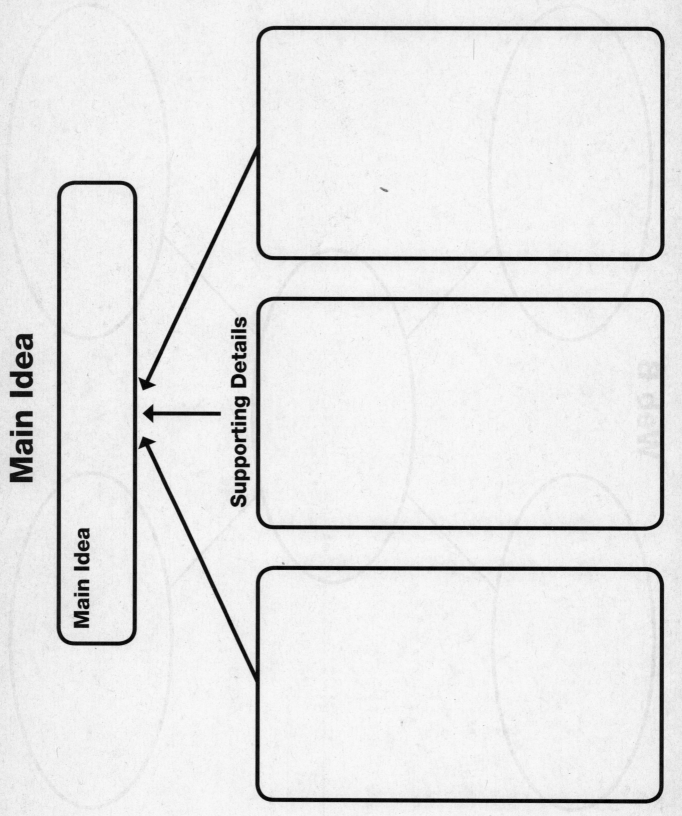

Main Idea

Supporting Details

Venn Diagram

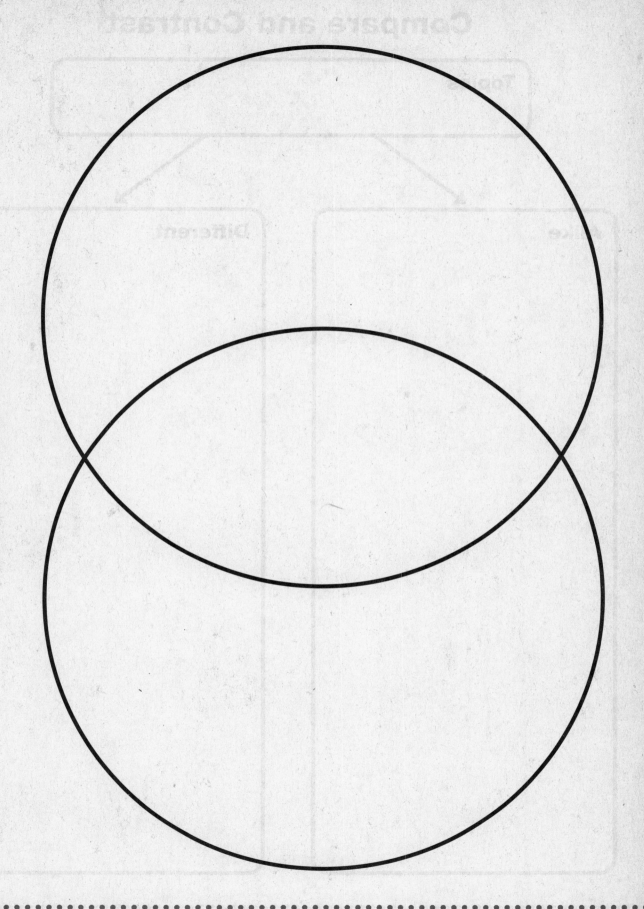

Compare and Contrast

Topics

Alike

Different

Cause and Effect

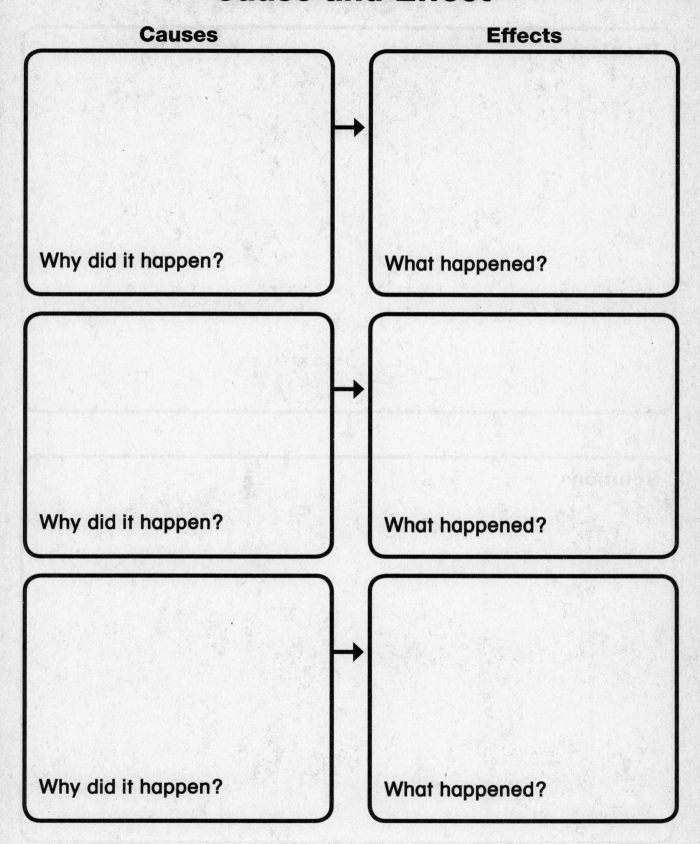

Causes	Effects
Why did it happen?	What happened?
Why did it happen?	What happened?
Why did it happen?	What happened?

Problem and Solution A

Problem

Solution

Problem and Solution B

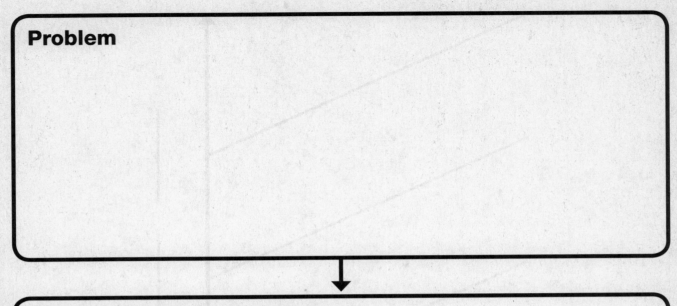

Problem

Attempts to Solve the Problem

Solution

Time Line

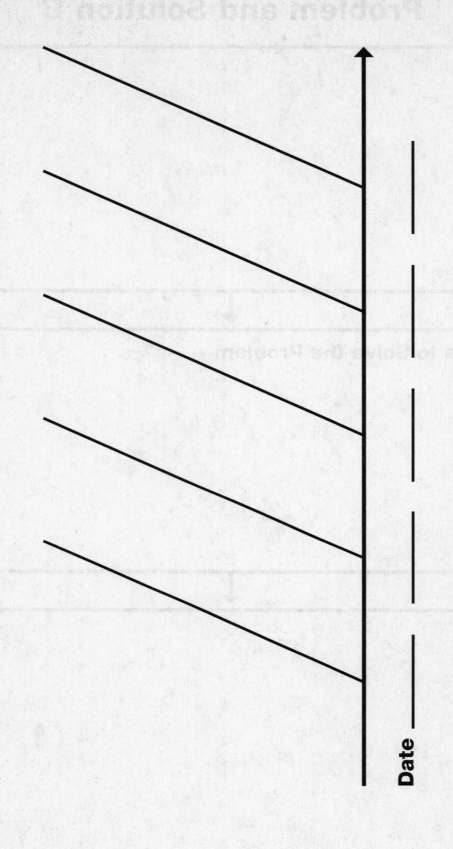

Date

Steps in a Process A

Process _____

Step 1

↓

Step 2

↓

Step 3

Steps in a Process B

Process _____

Step 1

↓

Step 2

↓

Step 3

↓

Step 4

↓

Step 5

© Pearson Education

T-Chart

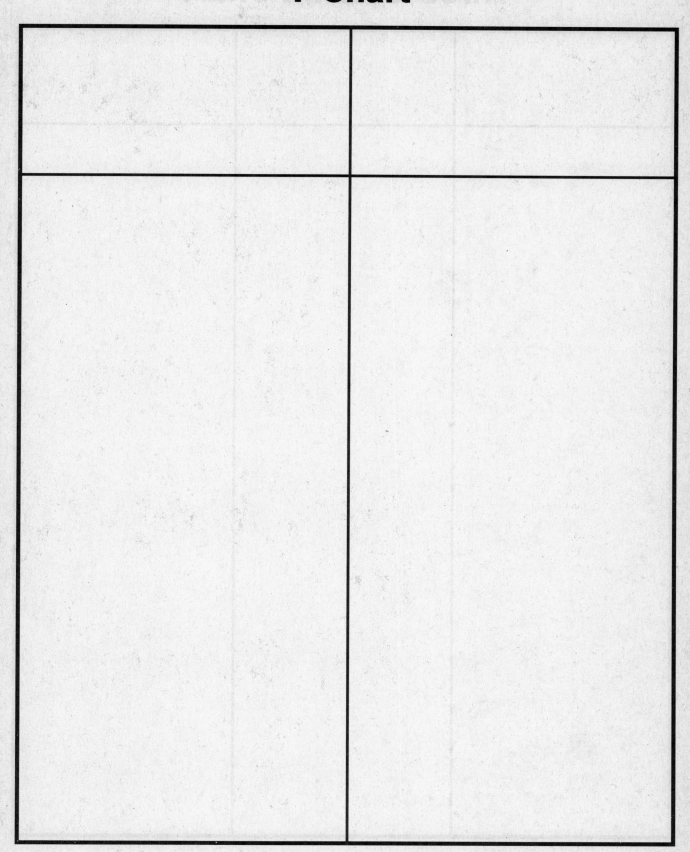

Three-Column Chart

Four-Column Chart

Four-Column Graph

Title _____

Cycle Chart

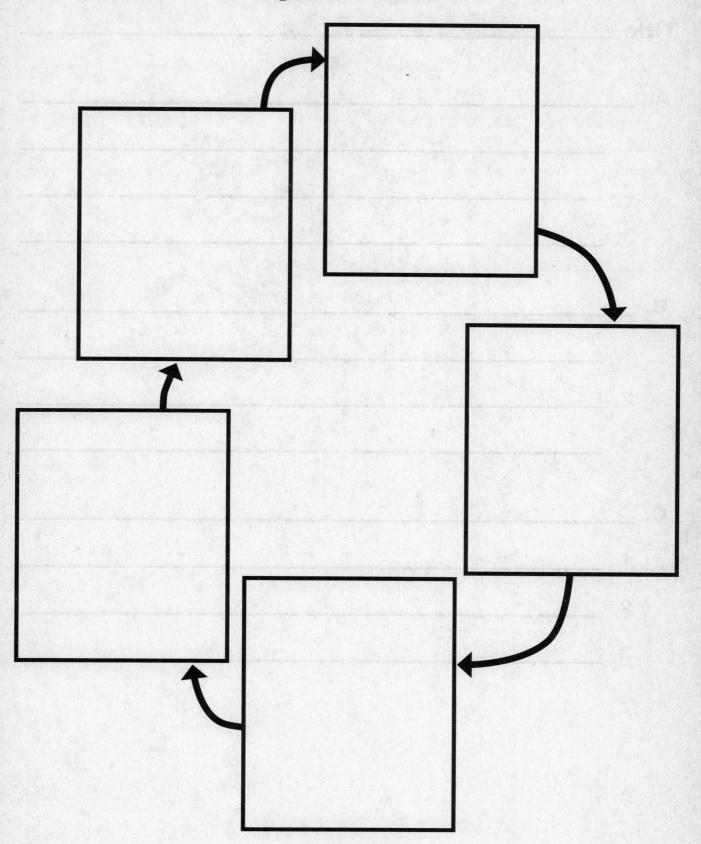

Outline Form

Title _____

A. _____

    1. _____

    2 _____

    3. _____

B. _____

    1. _____

    2. _____

    3. _____

C. _____

    1. _____

    2. _____

    3. _____

About the Graphic Organizer

Students use what they know as they preview the selection title, illustrations, and other text features.

Instructional Routine

This graphic organizer works well with any piece in which the title and/or pictures suggest predictions about a story conflict. It is simple enough for younger learners.

1. Direct students to the selection title. Suggest they preview the illustrations.

2. Encourage students to think about the title and the pictures as they predict a problem in the story. Remind them to use their personal knowledge and experiences as they think about a possible problem.

3. Have students check the accuracy of their predictions by defining one of the actual story problems.

Teaching Tips

- Before using this graphic organizer, discuss problems that have occurred in other stories students have read.

- Point out one particular piece of art that strongly suggests a problem. Model making a prediction.

Extensions

- After reading, have students identify similarities and differences between their original predictions and an actual story problem.

- Have students work in pairs to draw pictures that suggest a specific problem.

Skills and Strategies

- Predict
- Activate Prior Knowledge
- Draw Conclusions

About the Graphic Organizer

Students use what they know about the story title and selected words to make predictions about story content.

Instructional Routine

Use this graphic organizer with any selection in which the title and selected vocabulary words can help students make predictions about the story. The activity helps younger learners preview vocabulary words and relate them to the story.

1. Direct students to the selection title and present selected words from the piece.

2. Have students think about the title and the vocabulary as they predict what the story might be about. Remind them to use personal experiences and what they know about the vocabulary words as they predict.

3. Have students check the accuracy of their predictions by picturing a scene from the story.

Teaching Tips

- Before using this graphic organizer, discuss what students already know about each vocabulary word.

- Point out words that have more than one meaning. Help students predict which meaning will appear in the selection.

- After reading, have students compare their predictions with what actually happens.

Extensions

- Have students use each vocabulary word to write a question about the selection.

- Present groups with word lists (for example, *bicycle, lock, alley, forgotten, unfortunate*). Ask each group to predict a problem based on those words and improvise a skit built around the problem.

Skills and Strategies

- Predict
- Activate Prior Knowledge
- Draw Conclusions

About the Graphic Organizer

Students use what they know to generate interest in a selection and set purposes for reading by expressing what they want to learn.

Instructional Routine

The K-W-L chart works well with expository text. Young learners may need to brainstorm and suggest questions orally while you write the information on the chart.

1 Students brainstorm what they know or think they know about a topic.

2 Students list questions they hope to have answered as they read.

3 Students list what they learn as they read.

Teaching Tips

• If students need help with the K-W-L activity, work with them to generate a list of what they know and what questions they have about the topic.

• Suggest that if students are unsure of a detail they write in column 1, they can turn it into a question in column 2.

• Students can complete the K-W-L chart independently, with a partner, or with a group.

Extensions

• Provide student pairs with newspaper articles. Ask them to read the headlines and work together to begin K-W-L charts for the articles. Then have them read the articles together to complete the charts.

• Create ongoing classroom K-W-L charts as students investigate topics in other curriculum areas, such as science or social studies. You might file these charts by subject for students to use as references.

Skills and Strategies

• Activate Prior Knowledge
• Set Purpose
• Summarize

About the Graphic Organizer

Students focus on words one at a time and think about whether the words have any familiarity for them.

Instructional Routine

This chart works well with any list of words to be studied. Its simplicity makes it useful for younger students.

1 Students write a list of words to be studied in column 1.

2 Students concentrate on the words one at a time and put a check mark in the appropriate column. Column 2, *Know*, means that students know the word and can use it in a sentence.

3 Column 3, *Have Seen*, means that students have seen or heard the word but don't know or are not sure of its meaning.

4 Column 4, *Don't Know*, means words that are totally unfamiliar to students.

Teaching Tips

• Urge students to be honest in their ratings; at this point it doesn't matter whether they know a word or not.

• You can use students' completed charts as a diagnostic tool to determine which words students should concentrate on in upcoming study.

Extensions

• Consider the words that students rate *Have Seen*. If they are homonyms or have multiple meanings, discuss them.

• Have students revisit their charts after they have studied the words and make appropriate changes to their ratings.

Skills and Strategies

• Activate Prior Knowledge
• Recall and Retell
• Context Clues

About the Graphic Organizer

Students activate prior knowledge to predict word meanings and then cross-check predicted meanings with text context or reference sources.

Instructional Routine

The visual, step-by-step approach of the vocabulary frame works well with non-traditional learners who may find vocabulary learning difficult.

1. Choose a key word from the text. Have students identify ideas or symbols they associate with the given word and record these in writing or with drawings.

2. Have students think about what they already know about the word as they predict its meaning and write sentences using the word according to their predicted definitions.

3. Suggest methods students might use to verify word meanings. Encourage them to locate words in a dictionary or glossary or use context to check meaning.

4. Students use the word in a sentence with its verified definition.

Teaching Tips

• Model completing a vocabulary frame for one vocabulary word.

• Provide students with reference sources they can use to verify word meanings.

Extensions

• Ask students to note difficult words as they read a selection. Have them complete a vocabulary frame for each unfamiliar word.

• Each student can sign up to lead a group to complete vocabulary frames for chosen words.

Skills and Strategies

• Activate Prior Knowledge

• Predict

• Context Clues

About the Graphic Organizer

Students preview the selection title and illustrations and then predict what might happen in the selection.

Instructional Routine

This graphic organizer works well with any piece in which the title and/or pictures suggest predictions about the events in a story. It is simple enough for younger learners.

1. Have students look at the title and illustrations and then predict what might happen in the selection. Remind them to use their personal knowledge and experiences as they make their predictions in column 1.

2. Help students think about what clues they used to make their predictions and record the clues in column 2.

3. After students have read the selection, have them revisit the predictions they made. Have them write in column 3 what actually happened and then compare that with what they predicted might happen.

Teaching Tips

• Have students point out details and picture elements that suggest what might happen. Discuss *why* a picture gives clues to what happens.

• Have students talk about the personal knowledge they used to make predictions. This can include other stories they know of.

Extensions

• Have students discuss *why* things happened as they did and not the way students predicted they would happen.

• Have students change one story element—character, time, place, or event—and then discuss how the story would be different.

Skills and Strategies

• Predict

• Activate Prior Knowledge

• Draw Conclusions

About the Graphic Organizer

Students recognize the sequence of events in a selection.

Instructional Routine

This graphic organizer works well with any selection that has a clear sequence of events. It will help young readers begin to recognize plot structure.

1 Students record the title of the story.

2 Students record events that begin the story.

3 Students record events that take place in the middle of the story.

4 Students record events that end the story.

Teaching Tips

- Encourage students to visualize what is happening to see if the order of events makes sense.

- Remind students to look for clue words and phrases like *after* and *at last* to help them figure out the order of events in a story.

Extensions

- Invite students to draw cartoon strips with frames representing each section of their charts.

- Students might work in small groups to create sequence charts that map historical events from their social studies.

Skills and Strategies

- Sequence/Plot

- Recall and Retell

- Text Structure

- Summarize

About the Graphic Organizer

Students record the characters and setting of a story and track a sequence of events.

Instructional Routine

This graphic organizer works well with any selection that has a clear series of events. It can help students understand how the sequence of events affects the outcome of the story.

1 Students record the title, characters, and setting.

2 Students record events that happen *First, Next, Then,* and *Last.*

Teaching Tips

- Model identifying the sequence of events of a story.

- Remind students to look for the clue words given as well as words and phrases like *after, at last,* and *finally* to help them figure out the order of events.

- Students may not need all four boxes on the graphic organizer, or they may need to break down one box into more events. Help students redesign the graphic organizer accordingly.

Extensions

- Students can draw pictures of the main story events.

- Work with students to use a story sequence chart to map the events in a recent news story. Discuss how the order of events helped determine the outcome.

Skills and Strategies

- Story Elements: Character, Setting, Plot

- Recall and Retell

- Summarize

About the Graphic Organizer

Students identify the characters and setting of a story and a central problem; then they track a series of events that lead to the solution of the problem.

Instructional Routine

This graphic organizer works well with any selection that has a well-defined problem and a clear series of events that lead to the solution. It can help students understand how the sequence of events affects the outcome of the story.

1 Students record the title, characters, and setting.

2 Students describe a central story problem.

3 Students list the events that develop the story.

4 Students record the solution to the central problem.

Teaching Tips

- Model identifying the central problem of a story.

- Remind students to look for clue words and phrases like *after* and *at last* to help them figure out the order of events.

Extensions

- Have students draw pictures of the main story events.

- Work with students to use a story sequence chart to map the events in a movie or television drama. Discuss with them how the order of events helped determine the outcome of the situation.

Skills and Strategies

- Character
- Setting
- Sequence/Plot
- Recall and Retell
- Summarize

About the Graphic Organizer

Students write a summary of a story.

Instructional Routine

This graphic organizer works well with all types of fiction. It is especially helpful for guiding learners who are just beginning to explore story structure. Its prompts will help students organize their own writing.

1 Students fill in the blanks to identify story elements of title, character, and setting.

2 Students summarize plot structure by describing the sequence of events.

3 Students use clues from the story to write a statement of theme.

Teaching Tips

- Modify the graphic organizer to fit the specifics of a story.

- If students have trouble identifying the sequence of events, encourage them to return to the story and look for sequence clues such as *next, then,* and *after*.

- Identify the theme as the "big idea" of the story. Encourage students to use something from their own lives to help them understand this big idea.

- Remind students that sometimes a theme is not stated directly.

Extensions

- Students can turn their story elements graphic into story art. Invite them to draw pictures illustrating the setting, characters, and key events.

- Students might hold group discussions about the theme of the story and identify specific clues in the story that develop that theme.

Skills and Strategies

- Story Elements: Character, Setting, Plot, Theme
- Summarize
- Draw Conclusions

About the Graphic Organizer

Students analyze Author's Purpose and Author's Craft.

Instructional Routine

This graphic organizer works well with both fiction and nonfiction. Students analyze what was said, how well it was said, and how it might be improved.

1 Students fill in the title and author line. Then they choose a passage to respond to and write the page number.

2 Students summarize the content of the passage or write its main idea.

3 Students tell what they think is the author's purpose.

4 Students analyze how well the passage communicates and tell how they think it might be improved.

5 Students tell how they might express the same ideas.

Teaching Tips

- Students can work individually, in pairs, or in small groups.

- In Box 2, students can fill in one of the standard Author's Purposes: *inform, persuade, entertain,* or *express*—or use ideas of their own.

- Boxes 3 and 4 focus on Author's Craft—the language and structure the author uses. Check to be sure that students who criticize the author understand what they are reading.

Extensions

- Use the questions in Boxes 4 and 5 to explore vocabulary alternatives such as synonyms or variations on sentence structure.

- Students could also use this format to do peer criticisms of classmates' writing.

Skills and Strategies

- Recall and Retell
- Summarize
- Main Idea and Details
- Author's Purpose/Author's Craft

About the Graphic Organizer

Students summarize what they learned from a story or part of a story.

Instructional Routine

This graphic organizer works well with any kind of fiction. This form helps younger readers track stories they have been exposed to, as well as helps all readers better recognize and understand the elements that go into the making of a story.

1 Students record the title, author, and illustrator of the story.

2 Students record the setting and characters in the story.

3 Students think about their favorite part of the story, write a short summary of that part of the story, and draw a picture of that scene.

Teaching Tips

- Encourage students to visualize scenes from the story as they think about their summaries and illustrations.

- Discuss where the story takes place, what happens to the main characters, and how students feel about the book.

Extensions

- Invite students to draw a series of pictures in storyboard form of their favorite parts of the book.

- Have students look at similar stories to assess their interests in particular themes or authors.

Skills and Strategies

- Story Elements: Character, Setting, Plot
- Recall and Retell
- Summarize

About the Graphic Organizer

Students recognize the similarities and differences between two stories and make comparisons about text structures and story elements.

Instructional Routine

This graphic organizer works well with selections that have unique story elements but similar text structures. It is a useful way to compare selections within the same genre or by the same author.

1. Students choose two stories to compare and write their titles.
2. Students list the characters, settings, and plot events for both stories.

Teaching Tips

- Modify the graphic organizer by changing the items for comparison based on the stories being compared. For example, you might add space to compare Author's Style or Viewpoint.

- Students can use the graphic organizer to contribute to class or small group discussions.

Extensions

- To help students recognize their own writing styles, encourage them to complete story comparison charts for two stories from their own writings. Invite them to analyze their charts. Ask: Do you see common character types, settings, or themes?

- Suggest that students use the graphic organizer to compare one of their own stories with a story written by a classmate.

Skills and Strategies

- Story Elements: Character, Setting, Plot
- Text Structure
- Summarize
- Compare and Contrast

About the Graphic Organizer

Students explore their prior knowledge as they brainstorm related ideas, recognize concept relationships, and organize information.

Instructional Routine

This graphic organizer is appropriate for students of all levels and can be a useful tool for gauging their interests and prior knowledge of a particular topic.

1. Students write the topic or central idea inside the circle.
2. Students brainstorm words or ideas that relate to the topic and write them around the topic, connected to the center circle by the lines.

Teaching Tips

- Work with students as they list ideas. Encourage them to discuss how each detail relates to the central idea.

- You can use the web to determine where background knowledge needs to be supplied or what students are interested in.

Extensions

- Students might work in small groups to compare their knowledge of a particular topic with that of their classmates. Have students discuss where they learned about the topic.

- Students can extend this web by adding words or ideas connected by more lines to the secondary words or ideas.

Skills and Strategies

- Classify
- Summarize
- Main Idea and Supporting Details

About the Graphic Organizer

Students highlight a central concept and connect it to related words, ideas, or details.

Instructional Routine

This graphic organizer is appropriate for brainstorming ideas or relating details to main ideas.

1 Students record the topic or main idea in the center oval.

2 Students add related details and/or examples to the ovals around the center oval. (They do not have to fill in all the ovals.)

3 Students can add more ovals connected to the center oval, or they can add more ovals connected to the secondary ovals, as needed to explore a topic more fully.

Teaching Tips

- The ovals in this web are large enough to record more than one example or specific for each related detail.

- Use this web to explore main ideas and supporting details, character traits, vocabulary words and their synonyms and antonyms, or genre studies.

Extensions

- Encourage students to create a web that describes the traits of a literary character, family member, or friend. Invite students to write a paragraph or poem based on the web.

- Students can change the appearance of their webs by using circles, rectangles, or shapes related to their central topics, such as leaves.

Skills and Strategies

- Main Idea and Supporting Details
- Classify
- Summarize

About the Graphic Organizer

Students recognize a main idea and distinguish between the main idea and its supporting details.

Instructional Routine

This graphic organizer works especially well with a nonfiction selection that is organized around one main idea supported by major and minor details.

1 In the top box, students record a main idea.

2 In the remaining boxes, students list details that support the main idea.

Teaching Tips

- Help students identify the main idea by asking them to consider what the selection or passage is all about. The main idea is a statement about the topic.

- Remind students that not all details in a selection are supporting details. Tell them to include only details that tell more about the main idea.

- Point out that most well-developed main ideas will have several supporting details. Students can extend these boxes or add more boxes, as needed to explore the topic.

Extensions

- A main idea chart is a good way to help students plan their own written work. Students can record and organize details on the chart and use it as an outline for writing.

- Charting main ideas and supporting details can be a useful study method. Let students work in pairs to chart the main idea and details in a section of their social studies or science books and use their charts as study guides.

Skills and Strategies

- Main Idea and Supporting Details
- Summarize

About the Graphic Organizer

Students record similarities and differences between characters, places, ideas, or other elements of fiction or nonfiction.

Instructional Routine

A Venn diagram works well with any selection that lends itself to comparisons or contrasts between ideas or story elements.

1 Students label each circle with the name of one of the two things being compared.

2 In the circle with its name, students write details that describe that thing only. They do the same with the other circle.

3 Where the circles overlap, students write details that describe both things.

Teaching Tips

- It may be useful to look for details that describe similar attributes of the things being compared, such as size or color.

- Suggest that students look for clue words that signal comparisons and contrasts, such as *like, different,* and *however.*

- To make additional comparisons and contrasts, add more circles to the Venn diagram.

Extensions

- Students can create Venn diagrams comparing themselves to fictional or nonfictional characters they have read about.

- Assign each student an historical figure to research. Then have students work in pairs to create Venn diagrams comparing and contrasting their two historical figures.

Skills and Strategies

- Compare and Contrast
- Summarize

About the Graphic Organizer

Students record comparisons and contrasts in texts.

Instructional Routine

This graphic organizer works well with any fiction or nonfiction selection that lends itself to a comparison between ideas or story elements. Comparisons can also be made across texts. The graphic organizer can be used to explore comparisons an author makes or can help students make comparisons themselves.

1 Students record two or more central items or issues in the *Topics* box.

2 Students write the similarities between the two things being compared in the *Alike* box.

3 Students write the differences between the two things being compared in the *Different* box.

Teaching Tips

- Students can examine similarities and differences between various issues and items, such as characters or events. They can draw conclusions based on the similarities and differences they find.

- Remind students to look for clue words and phrases that signal comparisons and contrasts, such as *similarly, however,* and *on the other hand.*

Extensions

- Students could make real-life comparisons of two foods, two television shows, or two musicians, for example.

- Have student partners use *Spring* and *Fall* as topics and chart the similarities and differences in the seasons. Do the same for parts of the country.

Skills and Strategies

- Compare and Contrast
- Draw Conclusions
- Activate Prior Knowledge

© Pearson Education

About the Graphic Organizer

Students identify cause-and-effect relationships in either fiction or nonfiction.

Instructional Routine

This graphic organizer works well with any selection that has clear cause-and-effect relationships.

1 To record a cause, students answer the question, "Why did it happen?"

2 To record an effect, students answer the question, "What happened?"

Teaching Tips

• Even though causes come before effects in time order, it may be easier for purposes of study to identify the effects first.

• To help students identify cause-and-effect relationships, suggest they look for clue words, such as *so, consequently, therefore,* and *thus*. Remind them that there won't always be clue words.

Extensions

• Suggest that students use the graphic organizer to record important events in their own lives and to identify the causes.

• Students might work in pairs to list selection words that can clue cause-and-effect relationships.

• Often there is more than one cause for a single effect. Often there is more than one effect for a single cause. Ask students to choose a current event and brainstorm possible multiple causes and multiple effects.

Skills and Strategies

• Cause and Effect
• Summarize
• Text Structure

About the Graphic Organizer

Students identify problems and solutions presented in fiction or nonfiction.

Instructional Routine

This graphic organizer works well with all selections that clearly present a problem and solution. It is simple enough for younger learners.

1 Students summarize and record a problem presented in the text.

2 Students summarize and record the solution to the problem.

Teaching Tips

• To help students arrive at the problem, encourage them to ask questions such as "Who has a problem?" and "Why is it a problem?"

• Point out that a solution to a problem will not always be positive. For example, a problem might be resolved in a negative way, yielding an unhappy ending.

• With nonfiction selections, help students see how the topic sentence and supporting details may describe a problem and its solutions.

Extensions

• After they have summarized a certain problem in the first box, students might use the second box to suggest solutions of their own.

• Ask students to identify a local community problem and to create a problem-solution graphic organizer. They might use the organizer to write a letter to a city official or to the editor of a local newspaper.

Skills and Strategies

• Plot
• Summarize
• Text Structure

About the Graphic Organizer

Students identify problems and solutions presented in fiction or nonfiction and chart how plot events can relate to efforts to solve problems.

Instructional Routine

This graphic organizer works well with all selections that present a problem, various efforts to solve the problem, and a final solution.

1 Students summarize and record a problem presented in the text.

2 Students look for and record ways characters or people try to solve the problem.

3 Students identify and record the actual solution to the problem.

Teaching Tips

- To help students arrive at the problem, encourage them to ask questions such as, "Who has a problem?" "What is the problem?" "Why is it a problem?"

- Suggest that students look for words that clue the sequence of attempts at solving the problem.

- Point out that the first attempt to solve a problem is not always successful, and that a plot can be built around various efforts until one is successful.

Extensions

- After they have summarized problems and attempts in the first two boxes, students might use the third box to suggest solutions of their own.

- Students can work together to create a problem-solution graphic organizer for a problem facing their school.

Skills and Strategies

- Plot/Sequence
- Summarize
- Text Structure

About the Graphic Organizer

Students organize events from fiction or nonfiction in sequential order along a continuum.

Instructional Routine

This graphic organizer works well with any selection that presents events in sequential order. It can also help students understand and organize events that are told out of order.

1 Students record the first event on the slanting line and label it with the day or date below.

2 Students add the remaining events, placing them on lines relative to the other events.

Teaching Tips

- Remind students to look for dates and times of day as clues within the text and to notice words and phrases that signal a sequence of events, such as *first, then, next,* and *meanwhile*.

- Display some history book time lines and discuss how these graphic organizers aid understanding and recall. Encourage students to create their own time lines as study aids.

Extensions

- Students can create time lines to accompany reports on historical figures or events.

- Have students interview partners and create time lines based on important events in the partners' lives.

- Invite a group to chart important school events on a classroom time line.

Skills and Strategies

- Summarize
- Text Structure
- Sequence/Plot

About the Graphic Organizer

Students break down a process into three simple steps or else write a sequence of events or directions.

Instructional Routine

This graphic organizer works well with any procedure that has relatively few steps. If, as they work with this graphic organizer, students discover that a step really needs to be broken down further into smaller steps, help them redesign the graphic organizer to fit the situation.

1 Students write the title or a description of what this process will produce.

2 Students identify the first step, the beginning of the process, and write it in the box.

3 Students write the remaining two steps in the process in time order.

Teaching Tips

- Tell students to look for clue words such as *first, next,* and *last* to help them sequence the events.

- Suggest to students that before writing the steps, they try to visualize the process and the purpose of the process. By doing this, they will know where the steps are leading.

Extensions

- Students might complete the graphic organizer by drawing pictures of each of the steps in the process.

- Discuss with students the importance and usefulness of listing these steps. Have students brainstorm situations in which someone might need to follow this process.

Skills and Strategies

- Steps in a Process
- Sequence
- Visualize

About the Graphic Organizer

Students break down a process into simple steps. Students will be able to use the graphic organizer to recognize a sequence of events or directions.

Instructional Routine

This graphic organizer works well with any procedure that has more than a few steps.

1 Students write the title or a description of what this process will produce.

2 Students identify the first step, the beginning of the process, and write it in the box.

3 Students write the remaining steps in the process in time order. Adjust the number of steps as necessary to cover the process fully.

Teaching Tips

- Tell students to look for clue words such as *begin, first, next, then,* and *last* to help them sequence the steps.

- Suggest that before students write the steps, they try to visualize the process or the result of the process. By doing this, they will know where the steps are leading.

Extensions

- Students might complete the graphic organizer using illustrations or diagrams with captions.

- Discuss the usefulness of a list of steps like this. Have students brainstorm situations in which they might follow steps (following a recipe, assembling a toy, and so on).

Skills and Strategies

- Steps in a Process
- Sequence
- Visualize

About the Graphic Organizer

Students identify two items or concepts; explore and compare ideas, story elements, or vocabulary words; or chart ideas within a text and across texts, or between prior knowledge and new ideas.

Instructional Routine

This is a multipurpose graphic organizer that is helpful when exploring two concepts. It works well with all types of selections. Because the T-chart limits topics to two items, it is appropriate for younger learners.

1 Students head the chart with the two items being explored.

2 Students write or draw details in the appropriate columns, as needed.

Teaching Tips

• Students can use the T-chart to explore two story elements. For example, they might compare two conflicted characters or chart a problem and solution.

• Use a T-chart to organize ideas generated in a group brainstorming session.

• Use a T-chart to explore two vocabulary words. Listings under each word could include part of speech, pronunciation, definition, and a usage example.

Extensions

• Invite each partner of a team to complete one column of the chart.

• Students might use a T-chart to brainstorm pro and con ideas for a debate topic. Invite them to use their ideas to plan and present a debate.

Skills and Strategies

• Compare and Contrast
• Main Idea and Supporting Details
• Summarize
• Activate Prior Knowledge

About the Graphic Organizer

Students identify three ideas or concepts; explore or classify ideas, story elements, genres, or vocabulary features; recognize comparisons and contrasts; or chart ideas within a text or across texts.

Instructional Routine

This is a multipurpose organizer that is helpful for exploring and organizing three concepts of any sort. It works well with all types of selections.

1 Students head the chart with the three items or features being explored.

2 Students write or draw details in the appropriate columns, as needed.

Teaching Tips

• Students can use a three-column chart to explore story elements or genre characteristics.

• Students can use a three-column chart to organize ideas generated in a group brainstorming session.

• Use the chart to help students explore three aspects of a vocabulary word; for example, synonyms, antonyms, and usage. Model using the chart in this way.

Extensions

• Have students in small groups brainstorm topics that could break down naturally into three parts, such as *before, during,* and *after.*

• Suggest that student use a three-column chart to organize ideas in their own journals or logs.

Skills and Strategies

• Classify
• Main Idea and Supporting Details
• Summarize
• Activate Prior Knowledge

About the Graphic Organizer

Students identify four ideas or concepts; explore or classify ideas, story elements, genres, or vocabulary features; or chart ideas within a text or across texts.

Instructional Routine

This is a multipurpose organizer that is helpful for classifying information under four headings. It works well with all types of selections.

1 Students head the chart with the four items or features being explored.

2 Students can write or draw details in the appropriate columns, as needed.

Teaching Tips

- Students can use a four-column chart to explore story elements or genre characteristics.

- Students can use a four-column chart to organize ideas generated in a group brainstorming session.

- Use the four-column chart to help students classify selection vocabulary words. They can classify by parts of speech or categories such as *naming, descriptive, feeling, action,* and so on.

Extensions

- Students can use a four-column chart to plan a weekend's activities or organize shopping lists.

- Students might use a four-column chart to plan players or games for sports tournaments or playoffs.

Skills and Strategies

- Classify
- Compare and Contrast
- Main Idea and Supporting Details
- Summarize

About the Graphic Organizer

Students compare and contrast a variety of items, up to four in number; they can survey favorites or note tastes or trends within the class.

Instructional Routine

This graphic organizer works well as a survey or to determine students' prior knowledge. It serves as an immediate visual record of a variety of topics that have been quantified.

1 Title the graph.

2 Students add names or titles or draw or glue pictures in the bottom squares to identify what is being recorded.

3 Students collect data (possibly by surveying family members or other students) and color in one bar in the appropriate column for each positive response. The result will be a bar graph comparing the names or titles.

Teaching Tips

- Ask students questions about the information recorded, such as: *What does this graph tell you? Which is the class favorite? How many more students like (column 4) than like (column 2)?*

- Discuss what a bar graph is useful for: to display a visual comparison of the numbers of responses for selected topics.

Extensions

- Invite students to survey family members or friends about chosen topics and to display their results in bar graphs.

- Display bar graphs from other sources, such as social studies textbooks. Discuss the purposes of those graphs and how they are built in similar fashion to that of this graphic organizer.

Skills and Strategies

- Classify
- Compare and Contrast
- Activate Prior Knowledge
- Summarize

About this Graphic Organizer

Students record steps in a process or stages in the cycles of living things.

Instructional Routine

This graphic organizer works well with science or math topics. The graphic organizer helps students recognize the stages of life forms or environmental processes.

1. Student choose one box for the beginning stage. They enter the name, topic, or description, or they draw the first stage in the process.

2. Students follow the arrow to continue to the next stage, where they enter the appropriate name or topic or description.

3. Students continue around the cycle, making sure that the final stage leads back to the beginning.

Teaching Tips

- Students can write the stages of the topic and then draw them, if they wish.

- Suggest that before they begin writing, students plan how the topic of study returns to its original stage and how many stages it takes to do so.

Extensions

- Students can brainstorm a list of living things that might be applied to the cycle chart.

- Display cycle charts from another source, such as a science textbook, and compare what they show, how they show it, and how the information was assembled.

Skills and Strategies

- Steps in a Process
- Sequence
- Visualize

About the Graphic Organizer

Students use a simplified outline format to take notes on the organization of print materials or to organize their own thoughts before writing.

Instructional Routine

This simplified outline form is appropriate for use with younger students. Writers can change the outline to suit their own purposes, using as many main heads and subheads as they need.

1. Students record the title of the writing or a description of it.

2. On main head lines (*A, B,* etc.), students fill in the main divisions of the writing.

3. Secondary head lines (*1, 2,* etc.) are used to break down the main heads into their parts.

Teaching Tips

- Students can use topics, phrases, or sentences for their outlines. Once they have begun with one, however, they should be consistent throughout.

- Further divisions are shown with lower-case letters (*a, b,* etc.).

- Emphasize that an outline is a tool, and that students can revise and rewrite it as often as needed before they begin any actual writing.

Extensions

- Demonstrate how an outline works by doing a class outline of a piece of informative nonfiction from students' texts or materials at hand.

- Point out that certain kinds of books (social studies texts, for example) may have built-in outlines in the form of main heads, subheads, and numbered sections. These are meant to help readers understand the texts better by showing how they are organized.

Skills and Strategies

- Text Structure
- Summarize
- Main Idea and Supporting Details